STILL THOUGHTS
VOLUME ONE

By Dharma Master Cheng Yen

Translated by Lin Chia-hui
English Edited by Douglas Shaw

Translated by Lin Chia-hui
English edited by Douglas Shaw
Artist: Chang Su-hua
Cover Design: Chang Shih-ming

Published by the Tzu Chi Cultural Publishing Co.
Foreign Language Publications Department
Editor-in-chief: Liu King-pong
Address: No.19, Alley 7, Lane 217, Sec.3,
Zhongxiao East Rd, Taipei, Taiwan, R. O. C.
Telephone: 886-2-2898-9000
Fax: 886-2-2898-9889

Second edition, December 1996
27th printing November 2009
ISBN: 957-8300-47-6

靜思人文
JING SI PUBLICATIONS
http:// www.jingsi.com.tw

Contents

Part 1: The Dawn of Still Thoughts

Part 2: Questions and Answers
Section 1: Human Affairs

Section 2: Religion

Preface

In the thirty years since Tzu Chi was founded, the organization has increased from the original thirty members to four million today. Whenever I think of the Tzu Chi members, both in Taiwan and abroad, who abide by the principles of sincerity, integrity, trust and honesty, and who are engaged in the mission of helping the poor and educating the rich, my heart is full of gratitude.

In the last thirty years, many people have asked for my advice concerning all their problems. I have done my best to give them my suggestions. I have always believed that all living beings have the buddha-nature and their own innate wisdom. However, this wisdom is blocked by the poisons of greed, anger and delusion, as well as all other kinds of ignorance and worry. It is like trying to look into a mirror covered with dust.

I am grateful that people trust, love and support me. Their doubts are often dispelled and the evil thoughts in their hearts swept away by a couple of words from me. Actually, from my conversations with others, I have also received many valuable experiences and insights into life. I have compiled and edited these talks throughout the years into *Still Thoughts*.

The first and second volumes of the revised English edition of *Still Thoughts* will soon be published. I have especially asked the members of the Foreign Language Publications Department to do their best to use plain, simple English to edit these two books. Westerners who are not familiar with Buddhism may also understand the meaning contained in these books, and perhaps they may also receive a few insights.

Cheng Yen
October 15, 1996
Tzu Chi Cultural Center, Taipei

About Master Cheng Yen

Wang Chin-yun, now known as Master Cheng Yen, was born on May 14, 1937, in Chingshui, a small town in central Taiwan. Ever since she was young, the Master liked to engage in deep contemplation, asking where life came from, where people went when they died, and what people lived for.

When Master Cheng Yen was about 23 years old, her father died suddenly of a cerebral hemorrhage. Grief-stricken, she went to the temple every day and she began to think about becoming a nun. This was not an easy decision, since she was the oldest child in her family, her mother was in poor health and her younger brothers and sisters needed to be taken care of.

At the temple, Master Cheng Yen met a nun, Master Hsiu Tao, who became her mentor. Wandering wherever karma would lead them, Master Cheng Yen and Master Hsiu Tao stayed at several temples on the east coast of Taiwan. In 1961, this area was desolate and undeveloped and the people were poor. So, in a rather revolutionary break from Buddhist tradition, Master Cheng Yen and Master Hsiu Tao, believing that humans had enough suffering, firmly decided not to accept any donations from the local people. They raised their own vegetables, and earned some money by doing odd jobs, such as knitting sweaters and sewing baby shoes. In the winter of 1962, Master Cheng Yen affirmed her decision to become a Buddhist nun by shaving her head herself, a very untraditional act.

One day in 1966, Master Cheng Yen went to see a sick follower at a hospital in Hualien. At the hospital, she saw a pool of blood on the floor. People walked past it, not caring at all. Surprised, she asked, "Why is there a pool of blood on the floor?" Someone told her that an aboriginal woman living in the mountains had had a miscarriage, so the family walked eight hours to carry her to the hospital. When they got there, the hospital required an NT$8,000 [then US$200] deposit fee before surgery could be performed. The woman did not have any money, and the hospital did not want to take a risk either, so her family had no choice but to carry her back home.

When the Master heard this, she felt very sad. She wondered whether the woman would live or die, and whether her return would cost one life or two. And all because of the money. An overwhelming sadness arose in her heart. At that moment, she decided to establish a charity foundation to help the poor and educate the rich, because the poor lack material goods and the rich lack spiritual nourishment.

The Master began her work by asking each of her thirty followers, mostly housewives, to save fifty cents [US$0.02] from their daily grocery money. She fashioned little savings banks from pieces of bamboo and asked them to put the money in the banks before going to the market each day. With the motto of "fifty cents can also save people," word quickly got around every market in Hualien. More and more people participated and the program gathered strength. On March 24, 1966, the Buddhist Compassion Relief Tzu Chi Foundation was formally established. And thus a group of housewives carrying their grocery bags wrote down the first page in the history of Tzu Chi.

The work of helping the poor has developed on a broad scale. To this day, volunteers visit the homes of poor and sick people to cheer them up and see if they need food or money. Every month at the Abode of Still Thoughts in Hualien, Master Cheng Yen and her disciples distribute food to the poor. In the past three decades, Tzu Chi has helped more than one million people, both in Taiwan and abroad, and has distributed over US$68 million.

In 1979, Master Cheng Yen decided to build a hospital. At that time, she had nothing. Everybody told her that it was impossible. But she had the heart of the Great Vow Bodhisattva, who said, "If I don't go to hell to save other souls, who will?" This gave her great strength to do the impossible. The work of raising funds was difficult at first, but Tzu Chi finally received support from people at all levels of society. The Buddhist Tzu Chi General Hospital was finally completed on August 17, 1986. It was the first hospital in Taiwan that did not require a deposit fee and that directly admitted all emergency patients. Whether patients had money or not, they could receive prompt, professional medical care. Furthermore, the doctors, nurses, patients, and volunteers are like close family members. The mutual trust and sincerity between doctors and patients and the Master's principle of "great mercy even to strangers and great compassion for all" have made the hospital Eastern Taiwan's most moving legend of modern times.

Since then, Tzu Chi has also established a Junior College of Nursing and a College of Medicine to train caring, compassionate doctors and nurses. Master Cheng Yen does not only want good, skillful doctors. She also wants conscientious doctors who will treat patients for their illnesses and at the same time respect and care for them as they would their own relatives. So, in the College of Medicine, humanitarian studies are put on the same level as the medical courses. Tzu Chi has also established the Tzu Chi Taiwan Marrow Donor Registry, which now has the world's third largest data bank of volunteer marrow donors. Cooperation agreements with other registries in the world are being established in order to share information and increase the chances of finding a donor match.

The Tzu Chi Foundation continues to look ahead to the future. The foundation is currently planning to construct a disabled children's rehabilitation center in Northern Taiwan and a Tzu Chi branch hospital in Southern Taiwan. Tzu Chi is also planning to establish Tzu Chi University, which will be based on the College of Medicine, and which will include colleges of liberal arts, management, religion, and fine arts.

Buddha taught that religion transcends race, nationality, and geographical distance. Tzu Chi first began international relief work in the spring of 1991, when members went to help victims of a typhoon in Bangladesh. Since then, Tzu Chi has also helped victims of war and natural disasters in China, Mongolia, Ethiopia, Rwanda, Cherchen, Nepal, Cambodia, Thailand, South Africa and Guinea-Bissau.

Part 1
The Dawn of
Still Thoughts

1
The Best Moment Is Now

Time

- Every day is a new beginning of being a person, and every moment is a time for self-vigilance.

- Time can create character, accomplish work and accumulate merits.

- The length of a lifetime is measured by what one has achieved in that lifetime. Therefore, compete with time. Do not let it slip by unproductively.

- At every second, compete for goodness.

- During the times when we are free to do whatever we please, we are often deceived by this freedom into wasting time.

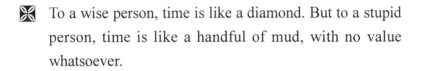 To a wise person, time is like a diamond. But to a stupid person, time is like a handful of mud, with no value whatsoever.

The Buddha said, "One only lives as long as one breathes." Human beings do not have the ability to control the length of their own lives, nor can they prevent their own deaths. Since this life is impermanent, we should cherish it, use it, and enrich it. Let the goodness, beauty and truth of this inconstant, precious life illuminate the true value of life.

Because our life spans are brief, life is even more valuable. Since it is not easy to be born in the world as a human being, we should ask ourselves whether we have developed our capabilities to the utmost during our lifetime, rather than constantly seek for longevity.

✠ One should be swift in doing good deeds, and one's meritorious deeds should be continuous. It is like boiling a pot of water: before the water reaches the boiling point, do not put the fire out, for it would be too much trouble to start all over again.

✠ Afraid of letting the days pass too quickly, we spend a lot of energy thinking of various ways to obstruct the passage of time. The only result is that we waste more time achieving nothing.

✠ Many people are obsessed with looking for miracles, and so are unable to go on in life. It would be useless even if these people had more time, an even longer path of life to walk on, for they would still achieve nothing in the end.

In the few decades of a life, the time to really be a person and actually accomplish things is very short. Even the most hardworking people achieve only one third of what they could do in a lifetime.

With nothing to do, we usually let time pass by idly. Life slowly passes by as we sleep indolently, so that our basic nature remains asleep for a whole lifetime. A person who lives like this can only be called a "sleeper."

Use wisdom to deeply examine the true meaning of life. Use perseverance to make the best use of your time.

The greatest difference between a saint and a common person is that a saint controls his own time.

�֍ Because life is so short, we should increase our stride and move forward quickly. We cannot afford to go through life as if dragging through a swamp, confused, muddled, and indecisive: "The front foot has already firmly touched the ground, but the hind foot is still afraid to let go." Instead, it should be that "After one foot makes a step, the other foot moves forward." This means that we should let go of yesterday's events and concentrate on what has to be done today.

✖ Regardless of how much pain and trouble we go through to accomplish something, we should not let our minds linger on past achievements. Regardless of how much we have given to others, we must not ask for favours in return or seek recompense. We cannot keep the past, and the future is difficult to predict. So seize the day, the moment is now.

✠ Abiding in yesterday, we produce nostalgic illusions. Constantly thinking of the past, we bring ourselves more pain, hate, anger and resentment.

✠ The future is a fantasy and the past is an illusion. We must protect the love of this moment, and carefully keep on fulfilling our duties at this instant.

✠ In life, not all balls are good ones. Only a seasoned slugger can make a hit every time.

2
Like the Moon, Like a Mirror, Like Water

Light the Lamp of the Heart

�֎ The heart should be like a clear moon: where there is water, there is the reflected moon. The heart should be like the sky: when the clouds part, there is a clear sky.

✖ Observe and listen to all living creatures of the world with a peaceful mind.

✖ The mind is like a mirror: even though the images reflected are constantly changing, the mirror itself never changes. The environment changes, but the mind never changes.

✖ When the mind constantly changes with external conditions, one gets confused by conflicts with other people and loses all self control.

�֍ When the mirror is used to examine and reflect objects, the mirror and the object must be placed a distance apart in order for images to appear clearly. When objects are placed directly next to the mirror or when the mirror has a dusty surface, then even the highest quality glass cannot reflect the object.

�֍ Our minds are like mirrors: if we desire wisdom and the ability to clearly judge affairs, we need to avoid worries caused by conflicts with others. This is what is meant by the old Chinese proverb, "Ones who are involved become confused; outsiders see clearly."

✷ Our minds are originally like mirrors: when facing mountains, they reflect mountains, and when facing water, they reflect water. But the ignorance of this world is like floating dust that distorts and obscures the reflected images.

✴ If we can always maintain a pure, clear state of mind, then everything we see around us will always be beautiful and good.

✴ People's minds should be like water, soft and supple in appearance, yet containing limitless power that cannot be stopped.

✴ The mind is like a field: if no good seeds are sown, nothing good will grow.

✴ Do not be afraid of heaven and hell. They are created by our minds and our actions. One should only fear getting off the right track.

❄ When the mind has no evil thoughts, one will always be able to feel at ease. When the mind is righteous, evil does not come near.

❄ By maintaining a good heart at every moment, every day is a good day. If we always have good thoughts, then any time, any direction or any location is auspicious.

❄ Commitments that accord with the proper principles should be broad and profound. Otherwise, even after thorough investigation of countless sutras and theories, the result will be like the moon in the water and flowers in a mirror, merely images without any substance. Nothing will be achieved.

※ Even if "every road leads to Rome," an indecisive and inconstant person who rambles on without concentration will not reach the final destination.

※ The mind is scattered and muddled in two ways: drowning in confusion and floating in movement. "Drowning in confusion" is to spend time foolishly and waste energy in laziness and sluggishness, unwilling to make progress. "Floating in movement" means to have an unsettled mind, creating thoughts that fluctuate endlessly at every instant. Without abandoning these two states, there is no way to be peaceful and tranquil.

※ Work hard. Don't worry and fret.

- Physical illness is easy to cure; mental illness is the most frightening. Those who have an illness of the mind cannot feel at peace whether walking, standing, sitting, or lying down. The whole body is uncomfortable; one has no appetite and cannot sleep.

- All people have problems: those who are rich and powerful worry about losing what they have, and those who are poor and weak fret about gaining what they lack. Worrying about gaining or losing just makes people upset.

- If one has nothing, then the mind does not encounter any obstacles. Without material possessions or the concept of gaining and losing, the mind is naturally free from obstructions. This is the mindset of the saints, and it is also the mindset that those who want to follow the Buddha aim to achieve.

If you regard others with a buddha-mind, then everyone you meet is a buddha. If you regard others with an evil mind, then everywhere you will see the flickering shadows of hideous demons.

Seeking illumination, some people light lamps. However, true light is in our minds. We do not have to go light the lamps in front of a buddha. More importantly, we must light the lamps of our minds

Because common people look for supernatural occurrences, their minds are in a state of confusion. Because their minds are confused, they go in circles, seeking eighty-four thousand ways to cultivate their minds. Actually, cultivating the mind is easy, for one only needs to abolish greed. People's minds are confused by greed.

❖ A mind that discriminates is defiled and biased. A pure, unbiased mind enables the buddha nature to appear.

❖ There is no difference between a mind, a buddha, and a living being. A buddha does not have one more hand or one more leg than we do. The only distinction is that a buddha's mind is clear and unencumbered, true and at ease. A common mind, however, is full of dust, the dust of worldly desires that gather layer by layer, obscuring our pure, true nature. A buddha's mind is like a safe which keeps the most valuable items. A common mind is like a garbage dump which has a lot of useless garbage that can never be clean and will only bring one suffering.

❖ The mind of an ordinary person is one that distinguishes past, present and future.

3
My Heart Feels Their Pain
Kindness and Compassion

- Compassion is sympathy. The compassionate heart is able to forgive, be patient, and express tolerance and love. The most fortunate people are able to forgive and sympathize with all living beings.

- Giving without thinking about the pain or trouble is "Great Compassion." To give one's labour and service happily is "Joyous Giving."

- If you rearrange the four words "joy, kindness, compassion and giving," then joyful kindness means to give happiness and teach the wealthy to share what they have, and compassionate giving is to relieve suffering and aid the poor.

- True, wonderful dharma flows out from wisdom. True compassion is motivated by the force of wisdom.

✖ Compassion is pure love. To have "great mercy even to strangers" is undefiled love. Though I have no relationship with a person, I can still care for him with a love that gives him happiness and brings me no worries. This is the greatest, purest love.

✖ Even though we have no relationships with other living beings, their suffering is our suffering, and their pain is our pain. When their bodies hurt, my heart worries. When their bodies are wounded, my heart feels the pain. This is called "great compassion for all."

✖ Regard others with a compassionate heart and give form to the abstract by turning theories into action. At every moment, bring forth the compassionate spirit of: "If we don't save them, who will?" If we can do this, even this impure world can turn into the Pure Land.

✵ Compassion is the origin of salvation, but without wisdom, it cannot become "great compassion." With wisdom, we can act with full perseverance and compassion. This is in accord with the Buddhist teaching that "compassion and wisdom revolve together."

✵ Love, humanity and morality are the essence of the compassion that the Buddha speaks of, and sincerity, integrity and friendliness are its functions.

✵ Those who can save others are called bodhisattvas. If what you put forth in one day has come to good use, then for that one day you are a bodhisattva.

✵ Give compassion a form with concrete actions.

The bodhisattva spirit is constantly one with the spirits of all living beings. In order to always keep the bodhisattva spirit present in the world, we cannot only depend on theories, but we must also have actual practice. Compassion and commitments are theories, and the work of saving people is true action. We must turn formless compassion into concrete, long-lasting deeds.

4
The Pure Lotus
Revealing Wisdom and Sowing Seeds of Goodness

- Inside every person's mind is a pure lotus flower. Everyone has limitless wisdom. Bring out the good side of your nature, and you will be rewarded with limitless blessings and wisdom.

- The Buddha came into this world only to teach people to be enlightened with a wisdom equal to his and to show them their inherent true nature. Everyone can cultivate compassion and wisdom.

- In learning to be a Buddhist, we must abide by the three principles which the Buddha taught: morality, contemplation, and wisdom. Morality guides the actions in our lives and disciplines our minds from doing bad deeds. If our actions are never wrong, our minds will have tranquillity and our spirits will become collected. Then we can develop wisdom.

⊠ When the mind attains tranquillity, wisdom will arise naturally. People are often being influenced by external circumstances, which shows that they are not tranquil enough. We learn Buddhism in order to achieve tranquillity. In today's usage, tranquillity means to keep calm and strengthen oneself.

⊠ Wise people come away from the experience of enlightenment with a good nature.

⊠ Most people think intelligence is wisdom, but this is not so. Intelligence does not necessarily include wisdom, yet wisdom contains intelligence. Intelligence is just an ability to measure advantages and disadvantages, gains and losses. Greed and deceit are signs of intelligence.

- Intelligent people have a strong sense of gain and loss. Wise people are willing to courageously part with all material and emotional attachments.

- As a result of their willingness to renounce all attachments, the wise gain. What they gain is unlimited happiness. Those unable to renounce their attachments will eventually lose. What they lose is their peace of mind.

- We grow wiser with every experience. Wisdom is tempered by the interactions between experiences and people. So if we avoid reality and hide from people and events, we will have difficulty producing wisdom.

- To be able to give love is a blessing, and to be able to do away with worries is wisdom.

- Wisdom and worry are like the palm and the back of the hand. Though both are on the same hand, the back of the hand is unable to hold things. But turn to the palm and the hands can do anything.

- Goodness is beneficial, and evil is harmful. With a single bad thought, one plants a seed of evil. With a single good thought, one obtains a good result.

- We must plant more seeds of goodness in the field of the mind. One more seed of goodness deters one more weed. If we do not plow and sow, weeds will flourish. Thus good deeds must be done daily, at every moment, continuously. Even the most simple actions need to contain some good thought.

- Do good deeds not because you search for fame and not because you seek merit. True virtue is accomplished when good deeds are done in the spirit of "I'm only doing my duty." This is the most selfless of all good conduct.

- The meaning of "good" is to be appropriate, just right, and not going off on deviating paths or being extreme. When we love others, we won't spoil them, produce anger or hatred, or discriminate unjustly in our relationships with others. With wisdom, we must eradicate the desire to possess the persons we love. With kindness, we must do our utmost to understand those we do not love and those with whom we do not get along well.

5
Undefiled Love
Improving Our Characters

- What is the most valuable thing in life? It is love. Those who make sacrifice a pleasure and who can give love will always be happy. Their lives will be meaningful.

- To love others and to be loved are blessings. Those who are able to love others or who are loved by others are fortunate.

- Don't close yourself off. You should love others first, and then others will love you.

- Only if you love yourself can you love all people.

- Take a step back when dealing with others. Be more generous when loving others. This way, you will be happy in the course of your life.

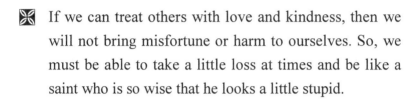

If we can treat others with love and kindness, then we will not bring misfortune or harm to ourselves. So, we must be able to take a little loss at times and be like a saint who is so wise that he looks a little stupid.

Turn anger into gentleness, then turn gentleness into love. In this way, the whole world will become increasingly perfect.

It is not only wealthy people who have the right to make donations. It is the right of anyone with a sincere and loving heart.

Definitely do not mix love with desire, because with desire there is defilement.

✠ The saddest feeling in life is that "others have their families, but I am alone." Therefore, those walking on the Path of the Bodhisattvas say: "When you regard all living beings, respect the elderly as if they were your own parents, love those of your own age as if they were your own brothers and sisters, and care for the young as if they were your own children." This is the truest, kindest, most beautiful, most sublime love in human nature.

✠ Cultivate pure, uncontaminated love and discard the emotional concept of "gain and loss." If we do not think of getting something back for our love, then we will not have any worries.

✠ Love that asks for something in return cannot last. What exists forever is formless, undefiled and undemanding love.

�֎ When parents love their children too much, the excess love puts pressure on the children. Do not be too concerned about your children, for only then will they be able to have peace of mind.

✖ A cup of tea smells and tastes good, and it gives you energy. But if the tea is too strong, it becomes bitter and undrinkable. Love in this world is the same way.

✖ Love. People often feel a lack of it in their hearts. They feel they can't get enough. When people crave love, they can never be satisfied.

✖ When talking about feelings, talk about long-lasting, enlightened feelings. When speaking about love, speak about great, unencumbered love.

- The Buddha encouraged us to have a great love that is deep and broad, filling the universe. Transcend yourself and unite your love with all nature.

- Every religious woman should cultivate her mind and body so she is like the moonlight, tender and soft. She should broaden her mind and shine the light of her wisdom. She should let her whole family, or everyone who comes in contact with her, feel like they were bathing in cool, refreshing moonlight. This way, she loves everyone and everyone loves her. She will attain the real meaning of love and improve her character.

6
The Fullness of the Rice Plant

Humility, Gentle Patience, Contention and Peace

�֎ The Buddha often warned his disciples not to be compla-
cent after attaining wisdom. One should behave like the
rice plant: the riper and fuller the rice grains, the lower
the rice plant bows down.

✤ A life lived with wisdom must have sincere humility.
With wisdom, one can distinguish between good and
bad, immoral and righteous. With humility, one can create a beautiful and satisfying life.

✤ The most important goal in moral cultivation is attaining
"no-self." Because if you can humble yourself and
broaden your heart to contain everything and respect others, others will certainly respect and accept you.

✤ Only those who respect themselves have the courage to
humble themselves even more.

40

- If you feel that even a small grain of sand hurts your foot, then of course you cannot cope with larger challenges.

- Some people cannot bow their heads in modesty, because they keep turning around to look at past achievements.

- To be humble is to have wisdom. To regard yourself highly is to have attachments.

- Not having money, one suffers. Having money, one still suffers. Whether bored or busy, one suffers. Who does not suffer in this world? Some talk about suffering because they cannot endure. Those who cannot endure suffer even more.

�֎ All living creatures have worries because they are attached to themselves. They are egocentric and think of themselves as the most important. This not only makes them suffer, but also makes others around them suffer too. Only by forgetting themselves can they create healthy bodies and minds and a happy attitude toward their spiritual formation.

✖ Love is a human power, but it is not sufficient by itself. We must also have tolerance: tolerance of insults, tolerance in yielding to others, tolerance in perseverance. If one is able to be tolerant, then one can be at peace.

✖ If you want to be welcomed and loved by others, first pay attention to your tone of voice and your behavior. Proper countenance, conduct, speech and deportment are all achieved through moral cultivation and tolerance.

- The basic work of moral cultivation is to have patience and to give.

- In Buddhism, our world is also called the "world of endurance." It means that one must be able to endure in order to live comfortably in this world.

- Endurance is not the highest state. When one no longer thinks about endurance, then one will feel that all adversities are natural.

- Adhere to the principles of integrity and sincerity in everything you do. Apply the attitudes of tolerance and tenderness in your conduct towards others. Maintain the tolerant mind and the accommodating attitude of the religious person in treating other people.

✖ The true saint is both tough and gentle. His toughness is found in his gentleness, yet his toughness contains gentleness. His gentleness comforts others, and his toughness strengthens his perseverance.

✖ If everyone can practice compassion and tolerance both at home and with all living creatures, the whole world will shine with true love.

✖ One should only compete with oneself for goodness and against time. When one competes with other people, then competition becomes a painful event and an unpeaceful word.

✖ Cultivate your own personality well and do not compete for honor. What you get from this competition is false, and what you obtain from moral cultivation is real.

✠ Competition is nourishment for harm. Wherever there is competition, there are distinctions of who is first and who is last. When one is concerned about gain and loss, and has difficulty in receiving and giving, nothing will be peaceful.

✠ Those who do not compete can see truth clearly. When there is fighting, there is confusion. When there is confusion, there is error. When there is error, there is failure. Nobody wins.

✠ People always have discriminating hearts and too many attachments. They draw clear boundaries between what is yours and what is mine. Then I fight for what I want, full of desire and jealousy. Consequently, I become narrow-minded and face obstacles everywhere.

- Most people say: "Fight as hard as you can." Actually, truly capable persons swallow these words.

- The majority of people compete with others for fame and wealth. If you can stop competing with others, everyone will have peace. When everyone has peace, the world will have peace.

- If you can maintain harmony with others, you can do anything.

- When people can live harmoniously together, there is no dispute. All lasting achievements in this world are based on the concept of harmony.

7

Adversity Is the Catalyst of Growth

Views on Adversity and Conflict

When adversity and conflict approach, maintain tolerance and forgiveness in the mind.

Nothing is very easy in this world. However, any circumstance that does not contain hardship is no good as a beacon for human life.

In Buddhism, adversity is called a "catalyst of growth." Feel grateful when confronted with adversity. It can be encountered but not sought after.

Hardships and difficulties in dealing with people and events are a kind of test. They are like swords that need to be ground on a whetstone to become sharp, or pieces of jade that need to be polished with a rough stone for their luster to shine forth.

- In order to cultivate oneself, one must be able to endure the hardships that discipline a restless mind into a tranquil one. Make the mind still in this whirling world

- Cultivate yourself second by second, minute by minute, day by day, and year by year. In everything we do, we must also go through endless hardships and challenges.

- People are usually imprisoned by the view of the self (because they often think only they themselves are right). They think that when people agree with them, there is truth, and when people disagree with them, there are disputes.

- If you doubt others, you cannot love others. If you suspect others, you cannot forgive others. If you distrust others, you cannot believe in others.

- The hardest thing for people to see is themselves. One assesses other people and criticizes worldly affairs without really knowing that oneself is also involved. Only when one can leap outside of oneself and make oneself an object of observation will affairs and theories be seen and distinguished clearly.

- Forgive those who harm people unintentionally. Do not be someone who is easily hurt by others.

- The more you distrust others, the less you believe in yourself. If you are negative about everything in the world, your belief in yourself will disappear.

- Let confrontation be a lesson, and take praise as a warning. Make rejection a self-examination, and see mistakes as experience. Any criticism is a valuable lesson.

✠ Others scold me, misunderstand me, slander me, and I am grateful. I thank them for giving me a chance to cultivate myself.

✠ A pure, upright mind is not afraid of being slandered. Be proper and sincere. Regardless of how others malign us, it is a chance to improve our characters even more.

✠ When wrong comes, turn it into right. When evil approaches, transform it into good. Solve any dispute with understanding, and there will be no dispute. When one hears any criticism, one should take it as a catalyst for growth in the process of one's moral cultivation. Never let criticisms accumulate in the mind as weeds of ignorance.

✠ If everyone could abolish arrogance, attachment to the self and ignorance, then there would be no disputes among people.

✠ Take disputes with others as an education. You can then turn undesirable events into instruments for reorganizing yourself. Don't take different viewpoints as disputes, for it will make your life miserable. In essence, all the minor incidents in life are living sutras.

8
Worry Is the Catalyst of Enlightenment

Beginning with Greed and Desire

✠ In this world, the roots of disharmony between myself and others or between right and wrong are greed, anger, and delusion. These three concepts produce endless disputes.

✠ Desire is a bottomless pit, and greed knows no boundaries. Once you want something, your mind will be set on getting it. If the mind is fixed on desire and gain, then there will be the suffering of loss.

✠ What is under the nose is even greater than the sea: a small mouth that can never be filled.

✠ With desire, there is change. With change, there is production. With production, there is destruction. Production and destruction go on and on, day by day, year by year.

✵ In life, those with great desires must use a lot of energy to satisfy their needs, while those with few desires have few worries and can go through life peacefully.

✵ If you get rid of your desires and lead a simple life, your soul will have incomparable peace and relief.

✵ Morality is reason. If desire continues to increase, it will bury reason. If reason can be enhanced, then it can end desire.

✵ Originally, all living beings got along with each other and lived harmoniously and peacefully. But this became impossible because we had too many desires. Because we are never satisfied and always try to get more, we have worries and increase bad karma.

✠ What we call "worry" is not measured by material possessions in life. Instead, it is only a state of the mind. If one cannot learn to be satisfied, one will always worry.

✠ Whether poor or rich, high or low, no one can avoid the suffering and worries of life.

✠ Everyone seeks "to have." What is "to have"? It is to have worries.

✠ Do not worry too much about the pain of illness. When you worry, there is no way to be relieved.

✠ Regard suffering as a challenge. Once you have overcome it, you will be happy.

- Forget the worries of the past and be free today.

- Learn to have a steady mind. With a steady mind, you will be truly self-possessed, no matter what situations or frustrations you encounter. You will understand that this is the way the world is, so you will not fear or worry.

- If you want to be always happy, then don't worry about the frictions between people. Some people are constantly troubled because when someone says something thoughtless, they take it seriously.

- If you broaden your mind, you will naturally stop worrying. Why do people worry? It is because their minds are too narrow to contain people whom they dislike or people who are more capable than they are.

- Losing your temper is both an internal and external problem. Internally, you produce anxiety. Externally, you trouble others.

- Take all the pain, difficulties, and worries as a good education. Each day is like a fresh page of a book, and the people, events, or worries that you encounter every day are the aphorisms and warnings that are written on it.

- It is through our troubles that we achieve wisdom. Only this kind of trouble is meaningful.

- Worry is a catalyst of enlightenment.

There is a Zen anecdote that shows how worrying and being frightened about common things are manifestations of illusion. When a Zen master was meditating, he suddenly saw a person with no head. The master said: "No head, no headaches." After he finished speaking, the vision disappeared. Not long afterwards, the master saw an image of a head and limbs with no body. The master said: "No heart and no stomach, no worries and no hunger." Then the image disappeared. Soon, an apparition of a person with no legs appeared. The master said: "No legs, no running about in confusion." The apparition vanished. Then the Zen master became enlightened: this world is illusory.

9
The Vastness of Heaven and Earth
Happiness and Wealth

�֎ There is no standard to measure happiness in life. If others are concerned about you and care for you while you are able to show concern for others and care for them, then you are blessed indeed.

✖ In this world, there are always others more unfortunate than ourselves. Those who are able to give their service are more blessed than those who are served by others.

✖ To forgive others one more time is to create one more blessing. The more one forgives, the more blessings one creates.

✖ We ourselves create all the offenses and blessings in our lifetime. Thus human beings are both the most terrifying and the most lovable creatures.

- Where there is a kind heart, there are blessings. Where there is commitment, there is strength.

- Cultivate your own field of blessings and reap your own good fortune.

- When your suffering is finished, fortune will come; when your blessings are used up, misfortune will come.

- Rather than seek good fortune and longevity, look for peace. To have peace is to increase good fortune and longevity.

- We are often advised to give, for giving brings more blessings than receiving. Real happiness is the purity, comfort, and happiness that comes after giving.

- The most ordinary person has the most blessings. He is content. He always cares about people. He is amiable and thus finds real friendships.

- The value of worldly materials goes up and down like the tide. During times of peace, gold, silver and gems are precious. However, during times of war and chaos, food and clothing are the most precious. The things that the world considers to be valuable are actually based on fleeting trends and vanity.

- Money is not an intrinsic part of ourselves, so naturally, there must be times when we gain and lose it. Thus there is no need to be proud of one's wealth or to be mournful over one's poverty.

- Common people seek wealth; saints seek truth.

If we think deeply about life, we realize that not a single thing accompanies us forever. No matter how much we love others and regardless of how much wealth we amass, in the end we must leave it all behind. Therefore, what else is there that we still cannot bear to part with?

It is not money that brings happiness. The mind with a clear conscience is most at peace. Being able to save, help, and give to others is the greatest happiness.

All the exquisite things in the world are illusions. They merely satisfy the common man's momentary vanity.

Those who are not hurt or beaten by their poverty and those who are not made proud or stingy by their wealth are all successful people.

Struggle to free yourself from your love and desire for material objects. With few desires and no greed, you will naturally feel free and easy and will lack for nothing.

10
So Light And Yet So Heavy

Your Voice and Expression When Talking

✵ People relate to each other using sound and facial expressions. Our voices should be soft and tender. Our expressions should be amiable and gentle.

✵ Say one inappropriate word and others will reject you. Speech should be just right. Do not speak too much or too little.

✵ Everything we say should be spoken prudently and unobtrusively. With close friends, one does not need to go into too much detail for them to understand. Strangers might not understand regardless of how candid and out-spoken one is.

✵ In teaching and guiding others, we should differentiate between those close to us and outsiders. With strangers, be gentle; with family and friends, be proper.

- If you have a bad temper and a foul mouth, then no matter how good your heart is, you are not a good person.

- We must listen and speak completely. Do not pick up the first few phrases here and the last few phrases there, and then put them together so as to hurt others. The resulting wound cannot be healed.

- Do not use your mouth to make trouble between people. Also, do not use your body for eating, drinking, merry-making, and indulging in material pleasures.

- Remember good speech like a sponge that completely absorbs water. Forget troublemaking gossip like a concrete floor, so solid that it still remains dry after water runs off.

✠ Dealing with evil speech and bad talk is one way to cultivate oneself.

✠ Do not cause friction with each other during disputes. Words weigh nothing on a scale, but if you are careless for even a moment, thoughtless words will press heavily on others' hearts. At the same time, train yourself not to be easily hurt by what others say.

✠ In everyday life, we should always be cautious of our attitudes and constantly reflect on ourselves. Always remember to treat others with magnanimity and speak to others carefully. This way, we can transform poisoned hearts and let all creatures live in peace and harmony.

✠ When one is calm, happy and clear-headed, one will be able to think clearly and speak appropriately.

If you look at people with your heart, you will not create conflict with others. Do not take other people's attitudes or words too seriously.

Your ears can hear all the sounds of the world, but you must use a sincere heart to listen to the good sounds which will help you to cultivate your morality.

If you are not truly sincere, you cannot keep a good heart. If you do not keep your word, you cannot put your words into action. The ancient sages said, "One can live without clothing and food, but not without sincerity and trust."

One word is enough, while a thousand words are meaningless. A significant word creates strong trust, and strong trust is very meaningful.

The beauty of human nature lies in sincerity. Sincerity is the origin of all virtuous ways. The value of human nature lies in trustworthiness. Trust is the basis of a full life.

11
The First Lesson on the Virtuous Mind
Quiet Thoughts on Repentance

�֍ Because of self-awareness, people grow. Due to self-satisfaction, they fall. Having a mentality that allows one to admit one's mistakes and criticize oneself is the first lesson of being a moral person, a step in sublimating one's character.

✖ As soon as one forgives oneself, one begins to get lazy. Be alert at every moment.

✖ To forgive others is a virtue, while to forgive oneself is to lose virtue.

✖ To courageously be responsible for one's mistakes is a good characteristic.

- Do not be afraid to do something just because you made a mistake before. Instead, correct the mistake, deal with the matter again and finish it.

- It is easy to think about one's big mistakes, but very difficult to get rid of small bad habits.

- Repentance is a confession of the soul, and it is also a major cleanup of spiritual pollution.

- How can a person dignify his life and thus respect himself? There is only one word: repentance. Repentance is to quickly acknowledge one's faults and not make the same mistakes again. A person who does this has real hope. Repentance also means having a sense of shame for one's mistakes.

✠ To repent is to expose your previous sins. To regret is to correct your past mistakes and cultivate for the future. Everyone has a conscience. If you are able to face reality courageously, examine yourself and repent, then you can be aware of your mistakes. Furthermore, if you sincerely confess, resolve to reform and do the utmost to walk on the path of righteousness, you can enlighten the mind, realize your true nature, and achieve purity and perfection.

✠ Since we are all ordinary human beings, how can we avoid making mistakes? As we progress from ignorance to understanding of the world, we all make mistakes, whether intentionally or not. We must repent all those mistakes. Repentance brings tranquillity, and tranquillity can get rid of all worries.

Every thought may affect your karma. When you are learning Buddhism, you should be careful not to make errors or conceal your evil. Otherwise, every time you open your mouth and move your tongue, or raise your hands and kick your feet, every movement will be a sin. At every instant, expose your faults and repent. Mend your old ways. You will then be unencumbered and peaceful.

 Always have quiet thoughts of self-reflection. Push aside the whirling confusion in the mind and discover the source of wisdom. Then, no matter whether you are actively cultivating your morality or pursuing a normal life in the world, you will be able to profoundly understand everything.

When a person is no longer able to educate himself, he is also unable to accept others' teachings. His development ceases.

12
The Strength of One Seed

Success, the Power of Commitment, and Maintaining Resolutions

Life is like walking on a tightrope. One should concentrate and look ahead. Walk forward and do not look back with empty regret.

The path of this life is not very long, but it is difficult to walk on. Thus we need to watch every step carefully. Do not go astray by walking in the wrong direction.

When you are young and strong, you charge into things enthusiastically, but you quickly run out of steam and become exhausted. Thus, you stop and go, already fatigued when the goal is still far away.

Success depends on the power of perseverance. Success is the accumulated fruit of long struggle. It is not based on a rash impulse or achieved in a momentary burst of energy.

⌘ Those who use their strength well do not hurry or hesitate. Those who hold to their ideals do not rush or delay. Progressing with firm, steadfast resolve, one reaches the goal in the end.

⌘ Those full of talent can easily achieve their goals and quickly obtain worldly satisfaction. On the other hand, because their desire has no limits, they will never be able to find inner fulfillment. Their talent becomes the root of their own suffering.

⌘ Our lives are not predetermined and cannot be completely comprehended. But our lives can be determined by our own commitments.

⌘ Everything originates from the seed of determination.

✠ If you are poor, you must not be poor in determination. If you are rich, you must be even richer in determination.

✠ In our lives, we should have a purpose, a commitment, an interest. Not having any purpose in life is like holding a pen without knowing what to draw. A dab here, a smear there... In the end nothing complete can be accomplished.

✠ Do not underestimate yourself, because human beings have unlimited potential.

✠ One should not regard one's own strength lightly. There is nothing in this world that cannot be done, and there is no one who does not have the ability. There is only the lack of willingness.

✳ When your drop of water falls into a tank of water, the whole tank becomes yours. This is because when your drop of water mixes with the water in the tank, there is no way to differentiate between what is yours and not yours.

✳ One cannot eat pictures of biscuits, nor can one string water bubbles into a necklace.

✳ We ourselves choose our paths. A thousand-mile journey begins with one step. A saint starts out by first being a common person.

✳ If you want to pick it up, pick it up completely. If you want to put it down, put it down all the way.

✠ One can acquire a bodhisattva's character only through one's own efforts.

✠ Cultivating a buddha heart has no far or near. People's resolutions have no great or small. With a sincere mind and proper resolve, any ambition can be achieved.

✠ In order to be the Buddha's good companions, we must learn to be great farmers. We plow the field of good fortune for the sake of all living beings in the world.

✠ An eager mind is easy to stimulate, a persevering mind is difficult to maintain. With only talk but no action, we do not realize the truth, nor can we practice Buddha's teachings. Only by maintaining the enthusiasm that we had when we first started to follow Buddha can we become enlightened.

The work of benefiting and aiding living beings requires three kinds of strengths: one is our own strength, the second is the Buddha's strength, and the third is the strength of equality.

Our own strength: Our strength is based on wisdom, blessings and karma. To receive good karma, we must first plant good seeds of karma ourselves.

The Buddha's strength: After we gain our own strength, we can rely on the Buddha's compassionate power and pray for the blessing of Buddha's merciful light. We hope to unite our minds with the Buddha's mind.

The strength of equality: The Buddha and living beings are on equal terms. The heart that respectfully makes offerings to all living beings is the same as the heart that respectfully makes offerings to the Buddha.

 Always getting up early in the morning is a good way to train oneself in the art of perseverance.

13
Life Is a Blank Sheet of Paper
How to Be Yourself

✱ Though grown on the same land and watered by the same rainfall, every blade of grass and every tree is different.

✱ Whenever living beings distinguish between things, they will have opinions.

✱ Every day in my life is a blank sheet of paper, and every person and every event are all vividly written essays.

✱ Everything in this great universe is a lesson for us to learn. Everything is part of the dharma and moral cultivation. Success is being willing to think, cultivate yourself and act with the utmost effort.

- Now that we are born in this world, we cannot leave the collective karma. We cannot leave society to hide from the world in our moral cultivation. True relief is acquired in our interactions with others and in the midst of our hardships.

- To appreciate others is to respect oneself.

- Everyone has a nature that can achieve buddhahood. By discovering one's own nature, one will have a concept of equality and will not make distinctions between "mine" and "yours."

- If you want peace, you must first have peace of mind. To have peace of mind, you must first act according to reason. With reason, you will have peace of mind, and then the whole family will be at peace.

�֍ If I understand one principle, I comprehend all principles. If I clearly comprehend all principles, know the way, and know what I am doing, then I will know myself. The most frightening thing is not knowing who I am, because then I will be confused and worried.

✖ Having a deformed body is not real suffering. Real suffering is having a deformed nature. Most of the disasters and calamities in this world are caused by people who have complete bodies and limbs, but incomplete minds and spirits.

✖ We must educate and reform all living beings by first behaving properly ourselves. Living beings are indomitable, and their minds and thoughts are inscrutable. There is only one way to reform a person: be proper and sincere. Sincerity and propriety can overcome the unyielding nature in living beings.

- There are three things that we should not depend on. First, do not depend on power. Second, do not depend on status. Third, do not depend on money.

- Use your time well, every minute and every second. By being practical every step of the way in this life, one will have no shame or regrets.

- Do not complain that people in this world are cold-blooded, utilitarian, and unjust. These situations are perfect opportunities for us to do something great.

- Only by doing what is difficult to do, giving what is difficult to give, and accomplishing what is difficult to accomplish can we sublimate our own characters.

- Reason shows us the way on the long road of life. When one is not familiar with the terrain, one will walk the wrong road. Thus in this life, one should study the terrain well.

- The Buddha brought his teachings to the world in order to teach all living beings to return to their true nature and to be their true selves. Therefore, if one has a complete character, one will have a nature like the Buddha. If one's character is incomplete, how can one attain Buddhahood?

- Say good things, think good thoughts, and do good deeds.

- Being without culture is like being in a desert under the burning sun without an oasis.

❖ This world is full of suffering. Being a person is also suffering, but it is the only way to become a saint and a Buddha.

❖ Interpersonal relations are the hardest to deal with. However, by maintaining selflessness and unattachment in every matter, one can continue on.

❖ Great joy means that at every moment one is happy. Joy has no jealousy, arrogance or anger.

❖ Personal freedom should be guided by morality. Social freedom should be guided by law. Otherwise everything will be too wild. When those with great strength, greed, and power act without restraint and the mind has no recourse, then there is no freedom.

- Do not let the shadow of unhappiness cover your heart. One must radiate light and warmth, so that life will be meaningful.

- The sunlight is strong, parents' love is strong, a gentleman's forbearance is strong, a common man's anger is strong.

- Smiling and frowning are both facial expressions. Cursing and talking are both utterances. Smiling looks better than frowning, and talking is more natural than cursing.

- If you look at the world from a different perspective, the world has unlimited magnanimity. If you treat people and events from a different viewpoint, everything becomes harmonious.

- Usually, when there is no trouble, I treat others very nicely. This, however, does not require any skill. When there is trouble and I am still good to others, then I have real skill.

- Even if this world were just a game, one would still have to be correct and proper. Do not be silly. Be cautious and do not fool around.

- Morality is a light for uplifting ourselves, not a whip for chastising others.

- One should be practical and honest as a person. A practical, honest person feels good.

14
Seeking Enlightenment
in the Workplace
Ways to Deal With Other People

- Labor is a form of physical exercise. Our workplaces are places for moral cultivation.

- When there is confidence, perseverance and courage, there is nothing in the world that cannot be done.

- One should do one's best and leave the rest to fate. Do not keep difficulties inside the heart. People must overcome difficulties and not be overcome by difficulties.

- The greatest achievement in life is to rise up again from failure.

- Life is impermanent. So when society needs you, act quickly. If you are still able to walk today, quickly take the first step and go.

- Be brave enough to roll up the cuffs of your pants and go into the water. Once you are standing in the water, you are already wet, so there is no need to worry about sweating or getting rained on.

- To be always mindful means that you concentrate on your hands when you are working, on your feet when you are walking, and on your mouth when you are talking.

- Regardless of what one does, one should take safety precautions in everyday life to prevent the unexpected. Do not underestimate the soft breeze or a weak fire. A little spark can get out of control like a prairie fire.

- Those with ability are controlled by others. Those who have talent and wisdom control others.

�֍ Wherever people do things, there are problems. If one wants to do anything, then one must first firmly decide to do it and not be afraid of the problems. When you are not afraid of problems, any difficulty can be resolved.

✖ Do not be afraid of carrying a heavy load. You can drive any car just by holding on tightly to the steering wheel. When you drive others across to the Pure Land, you yourself cross over too.

✖ Whether doing or being, one must progress vigorously. One should concentrate in order to complete any activity well. One can only progress by not being distracted.

✖ In the midst of the shouts for justice, how many cries for sacrifice are there?

Life is like climbing a mountain. You must find a good objective and use this temporary life to move towards it. Do not be lazy, because if you relax your attention for an instant on your way up, you will fall back down. Do not set your goal on many summits. Since each mountain is a different height, if you keep going up and down, in the end all your labour will be for nothing.

 Modern man is good at debating sophisticated worldly wisdom and fussing over every minor detail of his work. Most people only understand principles and nothing else. They are full of reasons and theories, but when they meet up with trouble, they do not know how to cope. This is the common person's mind.

 Social improvements are not achieved with slogans, but with actions.

- What is truth? Truth is when principles and reality are in harmony.

- Events cannot be without principles. Principles abide in the center, and all events revolve at the circumference. We must use principles to deal with events, and not the other way around.

- We stand between principles and events. When principles and events are complete, then we will be complete.

- Even if the Buddha were still alive, three things would still be impossible to change: the pre-existing karma of living beings could not be changed, living beings without the proper karma could not be enlightened, and the Buddha could not help all of them redeem their bad karma.

- One person cannot eat all the rice under heaven, and one person cannot finish all the work under heaven. Similarly, one person cannot single-handedly attain all the merits under heaven.

- In all activities, one should stand firmly on one's own principles. Do not try to please everyone. Otherwise you will lose your own principles and still be unable to help others.

- If you cannot influence others, just do your own duties well.

- Do not consider taking short cuts, for that small road you choose might be a dead end. Then you must return to the original road, and you will have taken a roundabout way for nothing.

15
When a Candle Tear Falls
Karma, Gratitude, Life and Death

- If your karma is strong, don't be afraid that it will come late. If you find the right path, don't be afraid that it is long.

- Any deed that is opportune is a good deed.

- When one has good seeds, one should grasp the proper moment and quickly plant the seeds in the earth. Furthermore, there must be plenty of sunlight, water, soil and air for the seeds to grow.

- All material objects are for our everyday convenience. Therefore we should cherish things and feel grateful and satisfied. This way, we will feel peace and satisfaction everywhere. We will be full of happiness and joy all the time.

- Some people keep their commitments in their hearts, but do not put them into action. This is just like plowing the field but not sowing the seeds. It is a waste of a good opportunity.

- No matter how good the opportunity or how great the rewards of good deeds done in the past, if one cannot make good use of the present opportunity, everything still slips away.

- Life is a stage. When one's predestined karma comes, there will be an unexpected scene in the play.

- An object has had a valuable life span when it is used to its full potential. If one does not cherish the object, but rather carelessly destroys it, then one extinguishes the life of the object.

- One should be grateful to one's parents and all living beings every day. During one's whole life, one should never disappoint them.

- It is rare that a person in desperate circumstances can still feel gratitude. But one who is always grateful will be less likely to fall into desperate circumstances.

- A Buddhist sutra says: "Life, is it really life? Death, is it really death?" Life and death, death and life, they are all part of the same cycle. Thus it is said, "Death is the beginning of life, and life is the beginning of death."

- A candle without a wick cannot burn. But if the candle has a wick, it still must burn to be useful. A lit candle sheds tears of wax, but this is better than not burning at all.

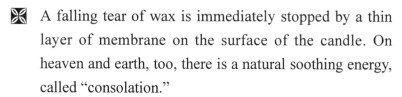 A falling tear of wax is immediately stopped by a thin layer of membrane on the surface of the candle. On heaven and earth, too, there is a natural soothing energy, called "consolation."

[The "candles without tears" made by the nuns in Hualien are wrapped with a special membrane. In Taiwanese, "consolation" is a homonym for the word "skin, membrane."]

The pain of birth and death are like a tear of wax falling from a candle. It is like being "consoled" by the "skin" of the candle after being hurt.

16
A Limited Life, an Unlimited World
The Path and Human Nature, Faith and Superstition

✠ Reputation and status, like the world's languages and writings, are abundantly colorful and tempting. However, because they have characteristics and forms and undergo many changes, they are impermanent and cannot be clung to.

✠ That which can change is not the true Path, but only a tool for moral cultivation. We should be able to accept it or let it go, using it well without being attached to it.

✠ What is the meaning of the saying "language blocks the Path"? When limited human life faces an unlimited world, what can be said and written is not as complete as it should be. When those who are resolute on following the Path depend only on language and writings to explain the Buddhist teachings, the Path is blocked. The true Path cannot only be passed on by writings or spoken in words.

To people who are practicing moral cultivation, sermons and sutras are like a ferryboat on the way to enlightenment. To reach the other shore, use this boat well. Upon reaching the other shore, do not be reluctant to put the boat aside to continue on the Path.

 The true Path is not reached by reading sutras or listening to sermons. Other than these, one must put what one has learned into practice. Only through actual practice can one understand the true Path.

 Before becoming Buddhists, some people do not believe in heaven and hell, and continuously strive to satisfy their longing for enjoyment even when they hurt others and themselves. Once they believe in Buddhism, they become obsessed with heaven and hell and the desire for merits. Both of these situations are cases of "confusion."

Our habits are not our true human nature. Our true human nature is perceived, cultivated, and brought into harmony through our habits. This is what we call "spiritual awareness." It is the truth perceived with our souls.

Without form, the content cannot be fully expressed. The form, however, must be in accordance with the "Middle Way" of Buddhism. It must be neither wild nor chaotic. One especially should not overlook the principle that the "form and truth are one."

If we believe that everything "exists," there is confusion. If we believe that everything is "non-existent," there is an end. When one believes that all things "exist," one continues to be attached to one's illusions. When one believes that all things are "non-existent," then those attachments cease.

Most people are obsessed. Those who are obsessed with themselves always think that they are the best in the whole world, that only they are the most capable. We should trust ourselves, but we must not be attached to ourselves.

 One should nurture courage and perseverance in order to confront reality and accept every situation one meets with a joyful heart. Do not be so quick to pray to the gods and ask for divinations. When the heart is confused, there is suffering, because the self is helpless and out of control.

 To be without beliefs is better than to be superstitious. In following Buddha, one must turn confusion into wisdom. Let go of that troubled mind common to all living creatures and return to the pure, undefiled buddha-nature.

✠ It is better not to believe than to be superstitious. One should believe with wisdom. Believe wisely. Do not try to chase the wind and catch the shadow.

✠ One who believes wisely can deeply understand the spirit of Buddhism. One who believes superstitiously twists the higher meaning of religion.

✠ If one has true faith, then one cannot go wrong on the road of life. When one's beliefs are wrong, then it is impossible to work properly. With twisted concepts, one easily makes mistakes in one's work.

✠ Proper Buddhist teaching does not speak about miracles or supernatural powers. If you really have the desire, you can become like a buddha.

True religion is based on an honest heart. When the heart is honest, one becomes more lively, and then one will become more at ease. If one has superstitious beliefs, one's doubting mind will produce devils, and then one will pray to gods for divinations. If one's faith comes from divinations and fortune-telling in the temple, one will not be able to truly and deeply understand Buddhist teachings.

17
Immersed in the Source of Human Nature

Ethical Refinement, Moral Cultivation, and Meditation

✠ The beauty of the whole is in the refinement of the parts.

✠ One's refinement, one's good character, is naturally shown in one's dignity, whether walking, standing, sitting, or lying down. When walking, there is a way to walk. When sitting, there is a posture for sitting. When sleeping, there is a position to sleep in.

✠ Some people often complain that they are not beautiful or that they do not get along well with others. Actually, getting along with others is not based on one's appearance, but on one's character. Good character is something we have to work at.

✠ Take a step back. Yield to help others accomplish something. This is the way to cultivate your morality.

- People often mistakenly think of "moral cultivation" as a term reserved for monks and nuns. Actually, moral cultivation appears in everyday life, and everyone should practice it in their daily lives.

- To cultivate one's morality is mainly to cultivate the mind within and show it externally. Because the mind cannot be seen, the only way is to rely on the orderliness of external actions to show inner purity.

- There are two kinds of people who diligently practice moral cultivation. One is forced by the suffering of life to cultivate the Way in order to seek relief. The other cultivates his morality because he has found his true self, and his experiences and frustrations only cause him to be more firm in his faith.

To stay on the Path of the Bodhisattvas, one must vigorously practice "The Four Guiding Virtues": giving, kind words, beneficial actions, and identifying with others.

Giving: "It is more blessed to give than to receive." Those who want to be a bodhisattva should continuously give and not ask for anything in return. Give your intelligence, labor, wealth, and material goods joyfully, and people will live in peace and harmony.

Kind words: Speak softly and have a kind expression on your face. When people hear you, they will feel good, and when they see you, they will respect and love you. If you are sincere and honest and speak kindly, you will be able to sweep away conflicts, heal depression, turn swords into plowshares, and transform violence into harmony.

Beneficial conduct: Using the body, mouth, and mind to do good deeds for the benefit of all living beings and compassionately saving the world are boundless meritorious deeds.

Identifying with others: A bodhisattva exists for all suffering creatures. Since we live in this whirling world full of suffering and hardship, we should first purify our own bodies and minds as examples for others to follow. We should inspire all those who work and live around us and encourage all people to walk together on the Path of the Bodhisattvas.

 Moral cultivation is not exploring long theories, deep concepts or abstract ideas. Instead, it is to truly and profoundly understand the true essence of human nature.

 Depart for the next reincarnation while you are still alive. The Pure Land is here and now. The purpose of moral cultivation is not to go to the Pure Land after passing away, but to go to the Pure Land while alive. It is to become pure and compassionate in one's present life.

- You should cultivate your morality on your own and work hard to develop a clear, bright sense of consciousness. Do not hope that results will come by themselves even if you do not cultivate yourself.

- In the eyes of patients, a doctor is a living Buddha and a nurse is Kuan Yin, the Bodhisattva of Great Compassion. Thus the hospital is a place where great bodhisattvas practice moral cultivation.

- Meditation regulates the body, mind and temperament. It makes body and mind one and movement and tranquillity the same.

- For those who use time well, every moment is a good opportunity for practicing meditation, whether dealing with people or affairs.

- When speech, action and behavior are unified in the spirit and mind as one, this is true meditation.

- Most people think that just sitting on a cushion is meditation. Actually, the goal of practicing meditation is to cultivate purity of heart, sincerity of mind and tranquillity of temperament. Meditation, tranquillity and sincerity cannot be separated.

- The main purposes of meditation and contemplation are to concentrate the mind, recollect the spirit, nurture understanding, and reflect on the nature of the inner mind. We do these in order to reflect on the past, carefully think about the present, and be alert to tomorrow. This also means to stop doing evil deeds and to do good deeds. Meditation is nothing other than this, so if one is able to do this, one is truly cultivating one's morality.

- The meditation of orthodox Buddhism is called "samadhi," which means "contemplation." True samadhi, which is achieved through the discipline and training of everyday life, is one of the methods of moral cultivation.

- To practice real meditation is to abolish the worries and illusions of everyday life and to concentrate one's spirit and mind. When you are mindful of what you are doing now, your mind will be focused.

- To follow Buddha, follow the living buddhas. To practice meditation, first study meditation in daily life. When every action and thought in everyday life is done in meditation, only then is there true, living meditation.

18
Teaching Buddhism Without Sound
The Path to Follow Buddha

- To act like a buddha is to give without asking for anything in return and to cultivate one's speech and conduct for the sake of all living beings.

- The Buddha's teachings are not only about how to perceive the meaning of life and death, but even more about how to accommodate others and avoid disputes.

- If you want to act like a buddha, you must cultivate yourself to the point where no matter what happens, you do not have the tiniest complaint.

- If you wish to behave like a buddha, you should first understand the principle of the impermanence of all things. By thoroughly understanding this principle, you can control your own life and be your own master in all that you do, always progressing towards a brighter world.

It is difficult to act like a buddha without nurturing love and patience.

Whether or not one can act like a buddha depends on how one gets along with others.

Believing and worshipping the Buddha is not believing in an idol. Instead, it is believing in the Buddha's character and life goals. When we turn and examine our basic natures, we come to believe that everyone has the same perseverance as the Buddha. One only needs to be mindful to bring forth one's true nature.

To behave like a buddha, you should cultivate yourself until your heart is tranquil and your mind is observant. Then every grass, tree, flower, and leaf under heaven will be an image of the Buddha.

❋ Life is impermanent. With material objects, there is creation, existence, decay, and destruction. With the mind, there is becoming, being, differentiation, and cessation. With living beings, there is birth, aging, sickness, and death. If we can thoroughly understand these principles, then we will not need to dispute with others. When we stop arguing over who is right and who is wrong, we can naturally concentrate on the Path. Then our minds cannot be manipulated by people or events in life.

❋ One does not have to listen to too many sermons. Merely using one's body to act out a simple verse of the sutras is the true dharma, the true root of virtue.

❋ The dharma is like a river able to wash the defiled minds of living beings. The dharma is like medicine. It is only good if it can cure the disease. Joy is good medicine.

In acting like a buddha, there are three minds: the undifferentiating* mind, the penetrating mind, and the compassionate mind.

[*A mind which does not make distinctions between good or bad, high or low, rich or poor, etc., but which treats all people or events equally.]

Before you begin to act like a buddha, your life is like a blank sheet of paper that you fill with scribbling going in every direction: you let yourself do whatever you desire. After you begin to act like a buddha, your life is like learning to write neatly and clearly: you must be proper and well-ordered in dealing with other people.

At every moment, the world is teaching dharma to us. This kind of dharma is without sound. Sometimes, it is even deeper than sound.

When living beings look for medicine, there is not one blade of grass nor one tree in the mountains that is not herbal medicine. But when not sought after by living beings, even the most expensive herb is not regarded as medicine. The dharma is the same. No sutras are too deep or too shallow. There is no high or low, no big or small. If the minds of living beings can absorb and use it, it is excellent dharma.

Part 2
Questions and Answers

Section 1: Human Affairs

Goodness and Beauty

What is goodness?

Goodness is wisdom. It is wisdom in judgment and wisdom of equality. With wisdom comes goodness and beauty. Goodness cannot be carried out with authority and power. This means that we cannot use "goodness" as an excuse to impose our opinions on others.

What is the relationship between compassion and goodness?

With only compassion but no wisdom, problems may arise. The most simple example is that kindhearted people are often swindled by others. Lacking wisdom, compassion fails to reach the ideal goals of goodness. Instead, it only aids and abets the swindlers. We must bring forth compassion within wisdom in order to have true goodness.

What is the most beautiful? What is the most joyful?

Tranquillity is the most beautiful and peace is the most joyful. This is the most beautiful, the most joyful, the most sublime attainment of practicing meditation, cultivating one's morality, and nurturing one's nature.

In this world, is there really anything complete and perfect? Can we seek perfection?

When there is a beginning, there is an end. When there is production, there is destruction. The search for material goods and fame is difficult and useless. There is no end to it and there is no guarantee. From this we can see that nothing is perfect in this world. We can, however, search for a complete human nature. This is a search for values, which can help us cultivate and improve our true nature and morality and let us reflect on our own personal perfection. Through personal cultivation and efforts, we can find our values and a perfect attitude toward life.

What kind of person is the most beautiful?

The most beautiful face is the one with a smile. A smile is an international language, an expression of love.

Morality and Conduct

What is morality?

Morality is a commitment to put one's skills to use in perfecting the Buddhist Path. When morality is in the mind but is shown externally through action, this is called the "form of morality." For example, one's way of walking, courtesy towards others, and so forth can show one's form of morality. Thus morality is the self-education, inner organization, and regularity that is expressed in external behavior.

A young girl asked, "How should we dress?"

It is best to dress naturally. Our clothes protect our bodies and express our characters. They should naturally suit our status, age and circumstances. To be beautiful, dress naturally. That which is too forced or unnatural does not look good.

What is speech karma?

When every word one says is true and one takes responsibility for every word uttered, one has "Right Speech." To do the contrary is to create speech karma. When one opens the mouth and wags the tongue, one always creates karma. Use wisdom to avoid creating bad karma. If one makes jokes or laughs at others, there will be an irrevocable retribution. Harmony and respect are the most important requirements for moral cultivation, thus one's actions should not go against the natural rules of life. Speaking to others with a vulgar tone of voice, lies, profanity or deception creates karma through sound, which is speech karma.

Why do we treat strangers more politely than friends or relatives?

Some people are very polite to those with whom they are unfamiliar. They observe every detail of etiquette and spend time together happily. But after they have spent some time together and have gotten more well-acquainted, then familiarity breeds contempt and they no longer think about courtesy. For this reason, some people say hate arises from love. In the beginning, when everybody is mutually polite, they are able to respect and love each other. But then, as they get to know each other better and their attention to etiquette gradually dies away, apathy takes its place. We should maintain the courteous attitude of the first meeting. This is the true way to be a person and deal with others.

Life

Since life is always aging, naturally there must be death. Does this mean that the basic nature of life is connected to suffering?

Life and death are linked together. The most painful thing about death is not death itself. The dead person already experiences no pain. Instead, it is the living who, spiritually threatened at the thought of death, feel the most pain. The suffering of death also includes the pain of parting with one's loved ones. One can't bear to leave all the things one loves in life, but yet must leave them. This is the greatest spiritual anguish. Because there is a day of birth, then there must be a moment of death. The suffering that we usually talk about is the suffering of the period of life between birth and death.

Often in life, right seems like wrong and wrong seems like right. Though we clearly know that everything in life is transient and vague like clouds and smoke, it is hard not to be upset by the conflicts before us. However, we must realize that from the day we were born as humans, we should be happy with our lives. We should learn from people like Lin Chen-chin. Some people asked him how he coped with both legs amputated. He replied, "I am much luckier than those who have injured their spines." We think he is suffering, but in fact he is not.

How should we view this world?

To use an analogy, when most people look at the world, the flowers and the grass, it is like seeing them on a piece of white paper. But when true observers see the flowers and grass, it is as though they were placed on a sheet of glass. What is the difference? Seeing something on a piece of white paper is only looking at a picture. One cannot see the whole environment of the flowers and the grass; seen by themselves, they are lifeless and alienated from reality. When one sees through the glass past the flowers and grass, one sees their natural background and their connection with all nature. They are flowers and grass, but they are not only isolated flowers and grass.

A young person asked, "Should we choose to live a plain, ordinary life or a risky, stimulating one?"

It is better to pick the ordinary life. Risk should be an action of last resort, so do not take risks just for the sake of taking risks.

One's life is only a tiny part of the universe. So what is really wonderful? What should be counted as stimulating? It is better to be ordinary and practical in everything we do.

Tolerance and Gentleness

Most people say: "When justice is on your side, you can speak strongly."

The Master says: "When justice is on your side, you should speak softly."

Most people say: "When reason is on your side, you do not have to forgive others."

The Master says: "When reason is on your side, you should forgive others."

What does it mean to say "When justice is on your side, speak softly"?

People need love. When one is too adamant, one loses love. Therefore, when you are right, you should be even more tolerant and gentle in order to extend your love and still uphold reason. Be a person who is friendly outside and proper inside.

If we act and speak strongly when we think we are right, what kinds of problems will arise?

When we think we are right, we do not stop contending until we win. If we insist too strongly, we hurt our friendships with others. The saying that "Those who have reason do not forgive others" means that we keep arguing to the end when we think we are right, because we are attached to our own principles. But this is wrong, for this is the way living beings create bad karma. Take all living beings into consideration. When we walk on the path of moral cultivation, we should also let living beings cultivate good karma. Therefore, when justice is on your side, speak softly.

I often feel very sad in my daily work.

Open the door to your heart! If you open the door, anyone can go in and out. On the other hand, if the door is too narrow, everyone will bump into it.

Master, when I am about to lose my temper, I think of the joyful heart that you speak of, and then I can suppress my temper. But when I have to carry that anger in my heart, I feel awful!

You feel bad because you still have to carry that anger. If you can nurture a mind that is joyful every moment and open your heart to accommodate everything, you will naturally have pure happiness and you will not feel so awful! This is a step-by-step cultivation, like a small stream of water that keeps on flowing. No matter how uncompromising or stubborn people are, they will be moved by your tenderness and goodness.

What is the kind, humble bodhisattva manner?

We should speak kindly and gently to the poor and our attitudes should be humble and amiable. The poor need love even more than material goods. Love is shown in our attitudes, so do not be arrogant towards them, but be kind and amiable.

Every time I visit victims of disaster and poverty and I see them so frightened and helpless, I don't know how to comfort them.

You should first use gentle, kind, loving words to warm their helpless, frightened souls. Then slowly establish religious faith in them, for when their spirits have something to depend on, those people can cope with the difficulties they face. Our work is not only to give them material help. Soothing their souls is more important. Helping people is urgent, but helping souls is even more urgent.

How can we tolerate others?

In the whole world, there is no one I do not love, no one I do not trust, and no one I do not forgive. If we can satisfy these three conditions, then our minds will be healthy and develop properly. Then we can naturally tolerate, love and trust others.

Forgiving Faults

A disciple was serving tea when she noticed a chip on the rim of the cup. She said, "Master, I am very sorry. This cup is chipped."

"Except for that tiny piece," the Master said, "the rim of the cup is still round, isn't it? Everyone has a shortcoming, but if you are not picky about that flaw, then the person is still a good person."

How should we treat criminals?

We should treat those who have done wrong the way the Buddha treats them. Forgive them, sympathize with them and help them, for there is a good seed in the true nature of all living beings. Actually, those who have committed offenses suffer more than those who were offended.

Do criminals feel bad about what they have done?

One who commits crimes is a prisoner in his own self-made hell. There are two instances in which the offender does not admit his mental suffering. In the first case, though the offender stubbornly refuses to confess his crime, he is actually very frightened. This kind of person is extremely weak inside and does not dare confront his own conscience. In the second instance, the person has psychological problems. He is already very sick, and he needs to be cared for even more. He needs love.

Because deep-rooted habits are not easy to reform, should we forgive those who habitually do wrong?

Deep-rooted habits are formed subconsciously over a long period of time. This is different from premeditated crimes. Thus we should naturally use even greater love and patience to educate and guide these people.

There is a story about a young monk. He had a difficult time correcting his habit of stealing, even though he wholeheartedly followed the Buddha. His master forgave him every time. However, in one case the circumstances were especially serious, and all the other monks were furious. They reported the situation to their master, demanding that the young monk be expelled. Otherwise they would leave, since they were ashamed to associate with him.

Their master answered: "Even if you all leave, I cannot expel him. Because you are diligent in your moral cultivation, you will be welcome wherever you go. But he has a problem and will not be welcome anywhere. So how can I abandon him in order to keep you all?"

All the monks were moved when they heard this. The thief felt ashamed and started sobbing with gratitude. He resolved to reform and finally become a new person.

What kind of person is happiest in this world?

Those who can forgive others are the happiest. As soon as you forgive others, your worries will vanish.

Putting Ideals Into Practice

How should we make commitments?

When you make a commitment, you must make it with your feet, which means to walk on the right path and stand firmly. Do not make your commitment with your mouth, all talk and no action.

A group of young scholars came to visit the Abode of Still Thoughts and asked the Master, "Why do scholars often feel annoyed?"

You are all intellectuals, full of knowledge from books. But when reality does not fit with your theories, you feel annoyed, for you only understand the principles, but not how to put them into practice. If you open your minds, do what needs to be done and leave whatever has to be left behind, then who will still have time to waste on meaningless annoyance?

One social worker lamented about the increasing chaos in the world and the degeneration of public morality.

Do not complain about how the world is now or how people treat each other now. Rather, we should strongly feel that because society is like this today, we need to do something about it even more. It is like when people are sick, they suddenly realize the importance of good doctors. These problems impel us to do something meaningful and call on us to actively help all living beings and put our ideals into practice.

Doing Work

A young couple asked, "What kind of attitude should we maintain towards our work?"

The Master said, "Sincerity and integrity."

They further asked: "But in our office, there is a lot of gossip."

"In this ordinary world, gossip and personal problems are everywhere. Gossip stops with the wise person."

When ordinary people are lost in gossip and disputes, what should they do?

The ordinary person is influenced by the law of cause and effect, constantly reaping what he sows. He is unable to escape from the karma of suffering that he created in a previous life. But the sage accepts his karma with a steady mind, thereby letting his own suffering quickly pass.

Most people often confuse dedication and capability, thinking that there is no difference between the two.

Even though capable people can act effectively, they still cannot avoid worldly habits. They can bear hard work, but cannot bear others' complaints. Dedicated people not only attempt to develop all their talents to the utmost, but even more importantly can endure both hard work and others' complaints.

Some people feel troubled because their responsibilities are too heavy.

Do not worry about having too many burdens or responsibilities. One who can face challenges will become strong. You only need to stand firmly, and your strength will grow greater and greater.

How should people regard rest and work?

"Rest" should merely mean another way of doing work. It does not necessarily mean to sit quietly without moving the body. We should make use of our human life more. With one more activity, we can complete one more job.

A disciple was helping to wrap candles, but she was very awkward. The Master showed her how to wrap a candle, completing the job in a blink of an eye. Everyone wanted to know how she did it.

Put your mind on what you are doing and your hands will move accordingly. You must pay attention to the details, concentrate, and do the work step by step. Don't do too much at one time. Work and moral cultivation are both done this way.

While some disciples at the Abode of Still Thoughts were working, they noticed that they were out of glue and borrowed an open bottle of glue from the Tzu Chi Foundation office.

About this incident, the Master said: "Every cent and every penny that Tzu Chi members contribute to the foundation is to help the poor. Therefore, not a penny may be misappropriated. If you need to borrow something, such as glue, then borrow a whole bottle and quickly return a new bottle. When things are perfectly clear, you can be accountable to the Tzu Chi members. Even small matters cannot be taken lightly."

One's Duty

A university professor felt saddened that education had changed for the worse.

In traditional Chinese society, the relationships between the student and the teacher under an ethical education system were honest and sincere. Everyone tried their best. But in today's utilitarian society, teacher-student relationships have changed. People are only interested in what they can get for themselves. They do not care about their duties.

Some people say, "This is my obligation." There are also people who say, "This is my duty." What is the difference between obligation and duty?

When people feel it is their obligation to do something, they do the job without paying attention to the cost. This is also the case when they feel it is their duty. However, obligation is "ought to," and duty is "must." Obligations are restraints. Duties are natural, a fulfillment of the inner part of you. The inner joy and individual awareness in each case are naturally different.

A graduate student who was doing volunteer work at Tzu Chi asked, "Which is more important, the means or the end?"

There should be a process, not a means. There should be a purpose, not an end. Process is a natural necessity. Means involves cunning and expediency. An end involves gaining and losing, while a purpose is a direction.

Responsibility

When young people see social injustice and unrighteous-ness, they want to be champions of justice. Is this kind of thinking and action appropriate?

They must first have the wisdom of contemplation. Fighting for the downtrodden and shouting about justice will make the situation even more complicated and confused. Many injustices are not as simple as they seem, so do not be too hasty to fight for justice, because you might just make things worse.

We should reflect on what we have done and what we are able to do. Everyone should try their best to do their duties. A sense of responsibility is more important than a sense of justice. If everyone acts this way, then there is a pos-sibility that society will become even more fair and just.

What is the difference between sense of responsibility and sense of justice?

A sense of responsibility is a demand on yourself, while a sense of justice is a demand on others. A sense of responsibility is a rational self-reflection, an offering of one's consciousness and talents. A sense of justice is an emotional outpouring, an impulsive response that may result in conflict with others.

When things do not go as they wish, common people get angry. What should they do?

You should immediately take hold of yourself and reflect. Anger is a lack of responsibility towards yourself, fruitlessly exhausting your body's physical and mental energy. It is an inner force of destruction that confuses the mind and destroys one's problem-solving ability. Achieve a state of strong concentration and face reality. Do not let reality disturb your mind's clarity and peace.

161

Communication

What is communication? How do we communicate with others? Can people with different habits and customs, lifestyles, backgrounds and levels of knowledge communicate?

Realistically speaking, the more similar our views, goals, and customs are, the easier it is to communicate. But it still depends on every individual. First, you must be calm and listen carefully, get rid of your own prejudices and have the wisdom to humbly accept other people's way of thinking. Then, you can really communicate. Communication is not having others communicate with me, but it is a question of how I can go and communicate with others. When you want others to yield to your opinion, this is not communication. This is only persuasion.

What is the source of the current traffic problems?

When human minds communicate well, the roads will also be smooth. It is a pity that every day, up and down the streets, drivers fight and argue. If we act this way, how can we use tranquil minds to communicate with each other?

Reform

I know I have many faults. I will slowly reform myself!

If you want to slowly reform, then you might as well not change at all! Life is impermanent and uncertain. How much time is there for you to waste?

Master, how come others who make mistakes do not have to reform, but I always have to reform?

Those who want to achieve buddhahood must reform. Those who do not want to achieve buddhahood can bicker with others a little more. One thought of enlightenment and one becomes a buddha. One thought of affliction and one is a common person.

It often happens that we are enlightened when listening to Buddhist teachings, but become confused when facing reality. How can we prevent this?

One should have perseverance and determination and make a resolution not to commit the same mistake twice. Always be alert. With courage when facing reality, one can achieve something great.

Poverty and Sickness

Why are nurses important and why should they take Kuan Yin's spirit as a guide?

Nurses play one of the most important roles in medical care. When people are sick, seventy percent of it is physical and thirty percent is psychological. Even with the best doctors and medicine, a patient still needs the nurses' care to be completely cured. Therefore, in addition to receiving professional training, nurses must also radiate the merciful spirit of Kuan Yin, the Bodhisattva of Great Compassion. Like Kuan Yin, they show compassion for those who are hurt and determination to save those who suffer. They express this compassion with unlimited concern and kindness.

Why is there poverty in life?

I tried hard to find the basic reason for this and discovered that poverty is often caused by sickness. One who has a healthy body is able to work and live peacefully. One who suffers illness eventually weakens the whole family. This is why of all good deeds, curing illnesses has the most merit.

Love

A young woman asked how men and women should love each other.

The relationship should be sincere and proper.

Is there a difference between true love and worldly love?

Worldly love tries to possess, while true love is sincere. With worldly love, one uses any means to achieve one's ends. With true love, one would rather make one's beloved happy.

What kind of attitude should a person maintain in order to help the poor with a caring heart?

When you give, do not consider the cost or the reward. In this way, you can reach a state of truth, goodness and beauty.

A man who was suffering because of love asked, "Can one stop loving?"

Love is difficult to stop. The Path of the Bodhisattvas enlightens all living beings; it does not stop love. Buddha's love is universal and undefiled; it does not stop love either. While worldly love and desires bring suffering to living beings, only pure, great love can free living beings from pain.

Even though today's children are doted on by their parents, they are still dissatisfied. What should be done?

Parents must create opportunities for the children to personally help do housework. Do not dote on your children, but instead love them with wisdom and inspire and guide them. Furthermore, use your parental love to care for and serve non-family members and all living beings. This way, our children can gradually understand the true meaning of love.

A social worker felt confused. "A friend of mine devotes herself entirely to serve society. However, she has no time to take care of her own family. There seems to be something wrong with this kind of person who loves all the people in the world but neglects those who love her most."

It does not just seem a little wrong. It is truly wrong.

A Tzu Chi member and his whole family went to pledge themselves as organ donors.

Being able to see through love and life and having no desire to possess, this is the love of the bodhisattvas.

Where can we find eternal love?

Look for it in your respect for people around you, look for it in the undemanding love that you owe to others, look for it in religion.

Mothers-in-Law

A young woman said to the Master, "I already treat my mother-in-law nicely enough, but she is not nice to me at all."

When your mother-in-law treats you badly, it is her business. But treating your mother-in-law nicely is your duty. You must know that your every movement is being watched and learned by your children. Since you are already ninety-nine percent good to your mother-in-law, why not be completely good to her?

How should parents-in-law treat their daughter-in-law?

When your children marry, you do not lose a daughter, but you gain a son; you do not gain a daughter-in-law, but you gain a daughter.

A Tzu Chi member asked how mothers-in-law and daughters-in-law should interact.

Be good to your parents-in-law. If you make them happy, they will not get sick. This will be a blessing for a son and a daughter-in-law. If you go against your parents-in-law and make them angry and ill, don't you still have to take care of them in the end? Care for and give blessings to each other. When you go to the market, do not think only of what your children would like to eat without a thought for your mother-in-law. In every matter, treat her with respect.

Raising Children

What is the most appropriate way to educate children?

Raising children is like growing trees. After you plant the trees, you must be careful not to add too much water or fertilizer, or else the roots will quickly rot. Nature already has the proper amount of water, sunlight, and air. It's the same way with children. The parents give birth to the child, but heaven and earth nurture him. On the other hand, if you spoil the child, you will hurt him.

Parents often worry about their children fighting.

They are just playing a kind of game. This is the beginning of children's social experience, and they might not think of it as quarreling. So parents should not be too concerned.

When children are naughty and will not study, what should be done?

Actually, parents can only fulfill their responsibilities towards their children. They do not have any rights over their children. Parents should plant more blessings for their children. Use a mother's care to love all living beings, and use the wisdom of the bodhisattvas to educate the children. Do not worry too much about the children, for this will give them bad karma.

A young woman's parents opposed her relationship with her boyfriend. The young couple encountered many obstacles, and in the end the boy married someone else. The young woman was heartbroken and considered becoming a Buddhist nun. Her parents, regretting the situation but unable to talk to her, came to see Master Cheng Yen for guidance.

Becoming a nun is a lifelong matter, like getting married. Both have to be done very seriously and cautiously. The decision to get married should not be based on passion or impulse. The decision to become a nun should be especially pure, clear and firm.

To marry is to enter another family. To become a nun is to walk into the Buddha's home and undertake the work of the Buddha. The work of the Buddha is caring for all living beings in the world. It is totally different from being a layperson.

This is a heavy, lifelong responsibility. If you could not take it, wouldn't you be miserable? Think about it carefully. Do not make a decision when you are confused or upset.

Raising a child is the parents' responsibility, but you must not be authoritarian about it. Do not expect your children to do everything you say just because you are the parent. This kind of love is too painful, too severe, and will even harm love itself. Wouldn't this go against your original intention to love and care for your children?

A medical school professor was pressuring his son to enter medical school, but his son did not want to do this.

You parents know that being a doctor is very meritorious and so you want your son to walk on this virtuous path. However, you must guide your children. Do not force them, for this will make them suffer. Even if you do it with the best of intentions, you may not get good results. You should be gentle and wise with your children. Let them go their own way.

Three New Year's Resolutions

On New Year's Day of 1983, Tzu Chi members inquired about Master Cheng Yen's New Year's Resolutions.

The Master's three resolutions were:

I will not seek to have everything go as I want. I only wish for enough courage to face reality.

I will not pray for health. I only hope to have a spirit filled with wisdom and a love that will never fade.

I will not look for fewer responsibilities. I only ask for even greater strength to do all the things that must be done in this world.

Questions and Answers

Section 2: Religion

Faith

What is the most dependable force in life?

No matter how rich you are, you cannot take it with you when you die. Regardless of how talented you are, there is no guarantee that your whole life will go smoothly. In real life, everything is illusory and unstable.

You must look for that dependable force in your faith. If you have faith, then no matter what circumstances or what difficulties you encounter, you will follow set principles and directions, going forward steadily like a ship with a compass on the sea.

A parent was troubled because his son had become a Christian.

You should be happy for him. To have a religious belief is better than having none at all.

A journalist lamented, "Why is it that I am always so busy with my work, running around and working hard without any rest, yet I often feel so empty?"

"You must first find yourself. Otherwise, you are like the duckweed that has no roots and floats on the water. Even though you work hard all the time, in the end it is all in vain."

He asked again, "How can I find myself?"

"Basically you will find yourself in religion. With the spirit of religion, your consciousness will be more concentrated, so you will not be deceived by the troubles of the world."

A man was a pious Buddhist, but his wife was a devout Christian. He asked, "With so many different religions in the world, how should people get along with each other?"

Religion should be like the great ocean. Rivers, small brooks and mountain streams all return to the ocean, which accommodates all of them. We should all have this ability to accept, appreciate, and love all religions. Act properly and do not haggle over who is right or wrong. Above all, do not say, "I am right, and you are wrong."

I often feel that society is unjust and feel that it is my responsibility to do something about it. I feel a lot of pressure.

Because people's views of life are different, their attitudes are also different. They all have the ability to judge what is right and wrong and good and evil in this world. But for the non-religious person who is concerned about injustice, the more he wants to correct injustice, the more pressure he feels. As for the religious person who wants to redeem all living beings from their suffering, he tries his best to do his duty. Thus even though his responsibility is just as great, he still has a kind, open attitude.

Both religious and political figures think that their own ideals are the best in bringing happiness to all living beings. Is there a difference in their views?

The true religious person has transcended the desire for personal gain, while the political person aims for personal benefit. Of course there is a very large difference.

Is there a difference between the ways that a Buddhist and a non-Buddhist practice their morals and lifestyles?

Buddhists and non-Buddhists are basically the same. They are all people, and they all have the same human nature and goodness. Even if a person is not a Buddhist, if he can develop his true nature and goodness, he can still do good deeds. But among Buddhists, there is a great difference between those "Buddhists" who act like buddhas and those who do not! Those who want to act like buddhas must wholeheartedly learn Buddha's compassion and behavior. Because saving and helping others become their responsibilities, they will often offer themselves in order to follow the Way, sacrificing themselves to achieve the goal of saving all living beings.

Those "Buddhists" who do not cultivate buddhahood will not be able to let go of considerations of their own advantages and disadvantages. Intentionally or unintentionally, they often reveal their desire to accumulate merits in order to gain divine blessings. On the contrary, those cultivating buddhahood seek no rewards for their good deeds. They are just like the Buddha who achieved buddhahood for the sake of all living beings, not for his own sake.

I have a lot of questions about Buddhism.

A Buddhist takes on the work of the Buddha and lets people believe with wisdom, not with superstition. We often hear people asking the Buddha to relieve them in their calamities, thinking that by worshipping the Buddha, they will be protected.

Actually, if we follow the Buddha and pray to the Buddha, we can use the profound teachings of Buddhism to activate people's belief, wisdom, and capabilities. Then we can let go of our attachments, so that we have the mental strength to progress. In sum, faith first helps us to reveal our higher consciousness, then helps us to awaken the higher consciousness in others.

A woman whose husband had been buried by a landslide had great difficulty bearing the pain of his death. She wanted to become a Buddhist nun in order to free herself from her grief.

There are young children in your family who need a mother's care and guidance. So if you leave them now, you will be irresponsible towards your children. This will increase your bad karma even more. You should do your best in your responsibilities as a mother.

Following the Buddha

Modern people often do not know the difference between the Buddha and a god, thinking that the Buddha is a god.

Buddha is not a god. However, all living beings in the world have the buddha-nature. The Buddha has transcended his human nature and become a saint. He is the most respected of those who are enlightened and who enlighten others. He is the guide of true human life.

Why can we make the buddhas saints but not gods?

Gods and ghosts are in the same sphere, because they still have emotions. Thus their reincarnations cycle through the Three Realms according to their karma. But the buddhas and bodhisattvas love all living beings like a mother loves her children, with no complaints or demands. Therefore, buddhas are saints and not gods. Gods are very distant from people, but saints are always by our side.

There are three kinds of Buddhist: one who acts like the Buddha, one who worships the Buddha, and one who believes in the Buddha. Which person is the true Buddhist?

The person who acts like the Buddha is the true Buddhist. We must emulate the Buddha's faith, perseverance, courage, and great spirit of self-sacrifice.

Why do we feel that Buddhism is so hard to understand?

If we go back to the Buddha's time, his teachings were not so hard to understand. Instead, they were truly accessible and understandable. They were principles for being good people in our everyday lives.

Because the Buddha's teachings were made so long ago and because people have venerated them, all sorts of special, esoteric stories were naturally added to them. If we can keep the attitude that Buddhism is a spiritual education for everyday life, then after we become Buddhists, we can obtain the truth of life.

Is it good for Buddhists to always go to temples?

Some Buddhists have minds that are like the ocean, never still, always giving rise to waves of worry. When some people first come into contact with Buddhism, they cannot wait to worship the Buddha and chant the Buddha's name, but they do not explore the real meaning of Buddhism.

If we want to behave like Buddha, we should act according to what he taught us and apply his teachings to our daily lives. An undiscriminating mind is a temple; an impartial mind is a temple; a penetrating mind is a temple.

How should we listen to Buddhist teachings in order to absorb them?

If you do not concentrate, you will not understand. If your mind is not composed, no matter how much you listen, you will not be able to comprehend. For most people, what they hear goes in one ear and flows out the other. Be attentive, then you will be able to absorb the teachings.

What are sutras and why should we chant them?

The sutras are the Way. The Way is the road. Chanting sutras is like looking at a map, remembering the names and the directions. By finding where we want to go on the map, we will know which direction to go.

Master, I really want to be a true Buddhist, but I can't read very well. Reading the sutras is really difficult!

The Buddha did not intend for us to take his teachings as texts that are only chanted with the mouth, but as a path to follow. When the Buddha preached, he was actually teaching the Way, pointing out the road for us. Therefore, we should vigorously put what he taught into practice in order to really be true Buddhists!

Merit

Are there merits in chanting sutras?

Some people think that if they merely chant sutras, the Buddha will protect them and relieve them in their calamities. This is a false concept. Living beings are confused and often lose their directions. The Buddha gave us his teachings to guide us in the direction that we should follow.

What is the meaning of chanting the Buddha's name?

There are many levels of chanting "Amitabha Buddha." There is the level of great wisdom, and there is the level of insufficient knowledge. Those with wisdom need only chant "Amitabha" once to absorb the limitless Way and comprehend Buddha's compassion. As for those who do not have enough wisdom, when they do not understand the meaning of the sutras, they must also diligently chant "Amitabha" to dispel bad karma and attain tranquil contemplation.

We often hear that if a person chants the Buddha's name thousands of times, he will go to paradise after he dies. Is this true?

That person is only counting how many times he chants, with his mind constantly on the numbers and not on the Buddha's name.

I heard that if you chant the "Diamond Sutra" three thousand times, you can break your attachment to names.

If you can break your attachment to names, only four verses will do it. If you cannot, then even if you chant the "Diamond Sutra" ten thousand times, it will be useless.

Cause and Effect

Please, Master, tell me the causes and effects from my past lives.

I do not know how to discern your causes and effects, but we must all pay attention to the law of cause and effect. We reap what we sow.

Why can't people control their lives? Why do we stupidly allow external conditions to order our lives, letting our fate arrange everything for us?

Only common people's lives are arranged by fate. Saints can arrange their own fates. How do we arrange our own fates? We need to have confidence, will, and wisdom. When we persevere in getting rid of our troubles, our wisdom will be brought forth and our karmic obstacles will be changed. You will be relieved and unencumbered.

Is there a connection between the law of cause and effect and our present conditions?

"Causes and effects come from the power of karma, but they will influence our present condition."

Another question: "Can we change the effects?"

"You must persevere in doing good deeds."

When will luck come?

As days go by, your luck will come. Be happy every day, and you will be unencumbered.

Superstition

Is it useful to have our fortunes told?

There is such a thing as fate, but you cannot become too superstitious about it. What most people call fate or luck is what Buddhists call karma. Since you believe in karma, then naturally there is fate. But in Buddhism, there is a saying that everything is created by the consciousness. Common people are controlled by fate, but the saint can control and manipulate his own fate.

My mother often goes to have our fortunes told and to ask about our luck.

If you have proper faith and proper concepts, then you can change your fate. Among our poverty cases, there are many who know how to tell fortunes.

A novice student of Buddhism came to ask: "Are there really spirits?"

Those who are unenlightened talk about spirits. Those who are enlightened talk about awakened consciousness.

Is there a connection between Buddhism and the supernatural powers that most people believe in? Many people think that devout religious believers are fanatics. Is this true?

The belief in supernatural powers, such as contacting the dead, communicating with the gods, or telling the future, is not part of Buddhism or Taoism. As for superstition, it depends on how people believe. Most people feel anxious and do not fully comprehend the true meaning of religion, so they believe in divination from the gods. Buddhism is not just a religion of worshipping idols. It is a religion that reforms human life and promotes science.

Often when people have business problems or become ill, they suspect that the household altar is placed inauspiciously or that some deity has been offended.

Buddhism talks about predestination and the law of cause and effect. If your mind is at peace, then everything is at peace. If your mind is at peace, then you will have no fears. In Buddhism, any position of the household altar is an auspicious one.

Moral Cultivation

How should we cultivate our morality?

In the instant of a thought. When you meet temptation, just pay attention to the thought of that instant.

A young Buddhist university student asked the Master how one should cultivate one's morality.

Every day is a new page in my life. Every person I see and every phrase I hear are the words and lines on the page. I comprehend Buddhist teachings in life, not life in Buddhist teachings.

What is meditation?

Concentrate on everything you do, whether eating or working. The mind without distractions is in meditation.

Some people feel that they have cultivated their morality well, but when they encounter one small problem, they get upset.

The common person's mind is easily churned up. The mind that the Eight Winds* cannot move can be moved by a light breeze.

[*The Eight winds are praise, ridicule, suffering, bliss, benefit, destruction, gain and loss.]

My heart is good enough, so why should I cultivate my morality?

Your heart is good, but who knows that? A true, good heart should be disciplined until good deeds are automatic. You should extend a helping hand without even the slightest hesitation. That is why there is a need for moral cultivation.

Two young Buddhist nuns came to the Abode of Still Thoughts and asked, "Master, on your path of moral cultivation, have you encountered any difficulties?"

The Master asked them in return, "What does 'difficulty' mean? I have never had time to think about difficulties."

"Haven't you ever had obstacles in relating with others?"

"Cultivating morality is something we do wholeheartedly. It is because we want to be free from conflicts with others that we need to cultivate our morality. If you do that but still provoke conflicts, then what is the use of it?"

One man said he liked to practice meditation.

To practice meditation is not just to sit. Whether walking, standing, sitting, lying down, carrying wood or hauling water, all should be done in meditation. We have to meditate in action, not just sit and do nothing.

Why should we observe the precepts?

Suffering, fear and anxiety all come from the feeling of guilt when one has done something wrong. To observe the precepts is to keep from doing wrong and to act properly in everyday life. If you make a habit of observing the precepts, you will naturally avoid doing wrong.

Supernatural Powers

Some people think that cultivating oneself until one can see spirits, buddhas, ghosts, and gods is the "Heavenly Eye Understanding." However, this is false thinking.

True "Heavenly Eye Understanding" is being unconcerned about worldly affairs and material things and refraining from bickering and fighting.

Some people learn to meditate until they can hear voices or sounds that others cannot hear. They think this is "Heavenly Ear Understanding."

True "Heavenly Ear Understanding" is to leave behind all worries, illusions and impure speech. One not only does not listen to gossip, but one can turn it into a lesson in Buddhism. All that is heard is the pure sound of Buddhist teachings. This is true "Heavenly Ear Understanding."

Some people think that people who have the "Power to Be Anywhere" can transport themselves anywhere instantly. Actually, this is impossible.

The true "Power to Be Anywhere" means that every road that one walks on in this world will be open. If we can maintain a righteous mind and a sincere attitude towards people and things, then there will be no difficulties in the world. Since there will be no difficulties in the world, then naturally every road will be open.

What is called "Knowledge of Past Lives" is to thoroughly understand the past, know the present, and predict the future.

If we want to know our past and future, we can see them very clearly now. There is a saying: "If you want to know your past life, look at what you are now. If you want to know about your future life, look at what you do now." Isn't this clearly telling us our past and future?

Are there people with the "Ability to Know Others' Thoughts" who know what others are thinking?

If we maintain a sincere mind that is always considerate of others and thinks of others, they will not have anything to hide from us. Then how can we not know others' thoughts?

Then what is the "Understanding of Purity and Disencumbrance"?

When you study Buddhism, do not keep praying to the gods. The most important thing is to cut off all troubles. After you become a Buddhist, you should develop the spirit of the bodhisattvas, and this is the true "Understanding of Purity and Disencumbrance" that we should all seek. If you can cultivate your morality until you attain this, then your mind will naturally comprehend all things. So why do you keep on blindly seeking these so-called "supernatural powers"?